CUTTING EDGE
TECHNOLOGY

Cutting Edge Internet Technology

ReferencePoint
Press®

San Diego, CA

Other books in the *Cutting Edge Technology* series

Cutting Edge Internet Technology

Bradley Steffens

ReferencePoint Press®

San Diego, CA

For more information, contact:
ReferencePoint Press, Inc.
PO Box 27779
San Diego, CA 92198
www.ReferencePointPress.com

LIBRARY OF CONGRESS CATALOGING-IN-PUBLICATION DATA

Name: Steffens, Bradley, 1955- author.
Title: Cutting edge internet technology / by Bradley Steffens.
Description: San Diego, CA : ReferencePoint Press, Inc., [2017] | Series: Cutting edge technology | Audience: Grade 9 to 12. | Includes bibliographical references and index.
Identifiers: LCCN 2016013750 (print) | LCCN 2016017512 (ebook) | ISBN 9781682820902 (hardback) | ISBN 9781682820919 (eBook)
Subjects: LCSH: Internet--Technological innovations--Juvenile literature.
Classification: LCC TK5105.875.I57 S755 2017 (print) | LCC TK5105.875.I57 (ebook) | DDC 303.48/33--dc23
LC record available at https://lccn.loc.gov/2016013750

Contents

Innovations in Internet Technology

1958
President Dwight D. Eisenhower founds the Advanced Research Projects Agency (ARPA) to expand America's scientific research capabilities.

1990
Tim Berners-Lee designs the first web browser and creates the first website.

1969
The first message is sent over ARPANET from the University of California–Los Angeles to Stanford Research Institute.

1967
Donald Davies presents his concept of packet switching, which is adopted by ARPANET.

1974
Vinton Cerf, one of the developers of TCP/IP protocol, coins the term *Internet*.

1960   **1965**   **1970**   **1975** ••• **1990**

1960
J.C.R. Licklider proposes building a network of connected computers that also connect to individual users.

1967
Scientists at ARPA begin work on a computer network called ARPANET, which eventually becomes the Internet.

1964
Paul Baran develops "message blocks" for network communications.

1961
John McCarthy describes a kind of public utility to provide computing resources to many people.

1996
George Favaloro coins the phrase "cloud computing" to describe data storage and software accessed over the Internet.

2016
More than 6 billion devices are connected to the Internet of Things.

2005
Chad Hurley, Steve Chen, and Jawed Karim launch the video-sharing website YouTube.

2002
Jonathan Abrams launches Friendster, the first social networking website to have 100 million users.

| 2000 | 2005 | 2010 | 2015 |

1997
The World Wide Web Consortium defines the first Resource Description Framework specification, a first step toward building the semantic web.

2008
Facebook overtakes Myspace as the Internet's most-trafficked website, with 116 million global visitors.

2015
More than 2.5 billion people use smartphones to access the Internet.

2004
Harvard sophomore Mark Zuckerberg launches Thefacebook, which later becomes Facebook.

2006
Amazon introduces the Elastic Compute Cloud, the first cloud infrastructure service.

Digital Disruption

The year is 2020. The place, New York City. A twenty-seven-year-old fashion designer named Eva is sitting alone at a restaurant, finishing her meal, when a message lights up her smartphone's display. "It is raining," reads the message. "Do you need a taxi?"

Not wanting to walk to the nearest subway station in the rain, Eva says, "Yes." Eyeing her unfinished dessert, she adds, "In ten minutes."

When Eva leaves the restaurant, a cab is waiting outside. She gets inside the car, and the driver takes her home. At the end of the trip, Eva does not pay the driver; he has already been paid. She gets out of the car and goes inside.

Pervasive Computing

Eva's story is an example of a pervasive computing experience. In this futuristic world—elements of which already exist today—machines communicate with other machines to simplify life for the computer user. The technological backbone of these communications is the Internet: a vast public computer network that connects billions of computing devices worldwide via fiber-optic and copper cabling, radio, and satellite signals.

In Eva's case, her intelligent personal assistant (IPA)—a software application, or app, residing on her smartphone—noted her location based on Global Positioning System (GPS) data sent from her smartphone over the Internet. The app correlated that information to incoming data about the weather, also received over the Internet. By mining a database of the times, locations, and weather conditions of Eva's previous taxi requests, the IPA found a high probability that Eva would request a taxi, prompting the app to ask if she wanted one.

When Eva said yes, the IPA "heard" her reply through the phone's microphone. The app then sent a message via the Internet to Uber, an on-demand car service that allows users to request private drivers through an app on their smartphone. The message included Eva's location and the time she wanted the ride.

Uber's dispatching software—not a human being—received the IPA's request. Using GPS data sent from Uber's fleet of drivers, the dispatch software sent Eva's request to the driver nearest to her location. The driver's smartphone display lit up with the request, and he arrived at the restaurant just as Eva was finishing her dessert.

pervasive

Existing everywhere and anytime.

When Eva reached home, the driver notified Uber via text message. Uber's accounting software processed the message and sent its own message to Eva's credit card company, asking it to pay the cab fare. Since Eva had already authorized her credit card company to pay Uber, the company's computer transferred the funds to Uber's bank account. Later, Uber's accounting software sent the fare to the driver's bank account. All the communications arranging and charging for the ride traveled over the Internet, and all were handled by machines—the hallmark of pervasive computing.

A Revolution in the Making

Eva's story is not a complete fantasy; many of the automatic machine-to-machine communications described above are taking place now. The only difference is that today Eva would have to contact Uber herself, rather than relying on her IPA to do so. Although IPAs like Apple's Siri and Microsoft Corporation's Cortana exist, they are not capable of making recommendations or carrying out orders such as requesting a cab. However, software companies are working on such advanced IPAs right now.

As Eva's story suggests, a revolution is taking place in the delivery of goods and services, a change known as digital disruption. Leading companies in many fields no longer produce or even warehouse products. Instead, they use the Internet to organize the delivery of products built by others. For example, Uber is

A woman uses a smartphone in a restaurant. In the future, smartphone apps known as intelligent personal assistants will form the backbone of pervasive computing, in which computers communicate directly with each other to simplify life for their users.

the world's largest taxi company, but it owns no taxis; the drivers use their own cars. Airbnb is the world's largest accommodation provider, but it owns no real estate. Facebook is the world's most popular media company, but it creates little of the content on its website. Netflix is the world's largest motion picture provider, but it owns no movie theaters.

Many cutting edge technologies will combine to make pervasive computing experiences like Eva's possible in the near future, including the Internet of Things, cloud computing, big data, and the semantic web. Some of these technologies exist today. Others are still emerging.

CHAPTER ONE

Web 3.0

The Internet has transformed modern life by making it easy to find, retrieve, and share words, pictures, music, and videos. The Internet also allows users to perform complex tasks such as filing tax returns, paying bills, and making airline and hotel reservations — all from their favorite computing device. They might use a personal computer (PC) connected to the Internet through a cable and a router, or they might use a laptop or tablet connected to a wireless router inside the home, in a library, or at any of the countless businesses that provide wireless hotspots. They might even use their smartphone connected over a wireless network or via their cellular phone network.

No matter what the device, the user does most of the work, typing letters and numbers into the computer and clicking a mouse or tapping a display to send the information over the Internet to another computer. In the near future, however, the computers will do more of these tasks, communicating directly with each other. Some experts call this next phase in the Internet's development Web 3.0.

The term *Web 3.0* describes an Internet usage model that differs from earlier models, known as Web 1.0 and Web 2.0. Web 3.0 employs a machine-to-machine model, meaning that an Internet user's computer communicates with other computers with minimal input from the user. This is different from both Web 1.0 and Web 2.0, in which the user engaged with the Internet manually.

Web 1.0

Web 1.0 was the earliest way of using the Internet. At the time, no one called it Web 1.0. It was known simply as going online or connecting to the Internet. The Internet user's computer, known as a client, would contact a remote computer, known as a server, over the Internet. The user would request information by typing a command into the computer or by using a mouse to click on a graphical user interface such as an icon or a link. This action would send a request in the form of packets of digital data over the Internet to the server. The server would respond by sending packets of data back to the client. Software in the user's computer, known as a browser, would assemble the packets of data into a viewable form—usually a web page.

One of the main characteristics of Web 1.0 was that most of the information the Internet user received was static. The web page might include something that moved, such as a slideshow or a video, but the content did not change. The video could be replayed, but sound and images remained the same. Everything the Internet user saw and heard on a web page was placed there by the page's creator. In Web 1.0 the people who built websites controlled most of the Internet's content.

> **cellular**
>
> **A communication network in which the last link is wireless.**

A few websites in Web 1.0 were not static. Websites known as bulletin boards and chat rooms—which still exist—allowed Internet users to post comments and other media to a web page. Chat rooms often served groups of people sharing a common interest, such as computing, gaming, or sports. Sometimes a person known as a moderator would review the posts before letting them appear on the website. Most of the time, however, the user's comments were posted without being reviewed. On bulletin boards and in chat rooms, Internet users created the content.

Web developers soon created applications that allowed people to chat online without being on a full-blown website. Instead, the chat would occur in a small window on the screen. Unlike chat rooms, where several people would chat at the same time, these chatting applications allowed two people to chat privately. This one-to-one online communication became known as instant messaging. ICQ, AIM, and Windows Messenger were popular instant messaging programs.

The Internet has transformed modern life by allowing users to perform complex tasks such as paying bills, purchasing movie tickets, and making airline and hotel reservations online. Here, a traveler checks in for his airline flight electronically at an airport kiosk.

Web 2.0

The chat rooms, bulletin boards, and instant messaging of Web 1.0 allowed people to discuss their interests and share pictures and other media in real time, but the websites were not pleasing to look at or easy to navigate. In the late 1990s web developers began to create attractive, easy-to-use websites that let people share information about themselves and socialize with others. Soon, websites like SixDegrees, Friendster, and Myspace allowed users to create profiles, invite friends, upload pictures, and share their likes and dislikes in music, movies, fashion, sports, and life in general.

Social networking websites grew at an astonishing rate. Launched in March 2003, Friendster was the first social networking site to surpass 1 million users. By the fall of that year, membership had rocketed to 3 million users. However, Friendster was soon overtaken by Myspace, which reached 100 million users by 2008. Myspace remained number one in website traffic until April

2008, when a new social networking website named Facebook logged 116 million global visitors, compared to Myspace's 115 million. The next month Facebook had 124 million visitors, while Myspace had dropped to 114.5 million visitors. Just one year later, the number of Facebook users had more than doubled, to 307 million. Three years later, in the fall of 2012, the number of Facebook users surpassed 1 billion. By early 2016 that number stood at 1.6 billion.

server

A computer that provides functionality to many devices.

The success of Myspace and Facebook inspired the launch of other social networking websites, each with a narrower focus. For example, Twitter, launched in 2006, allowed users to post 140-character comments, or "tweets," and to comment on and share, or "retweet," other tweets. Flickr, Instagram, and Snapchat made it easy for users to upload and share photographs and short videos. YouTube let users post both short and long videos.

Users Take Control

Unlike the content on most Web 1.0 websites, the words and pictures on social networking websites are created by the users, not by the website builders. The same is true of weblogs, or blogs. Bloggers write and post entries, often accompanied by pictures. Internet users also provide content for collaborative websites such as *Wikipedia*, an online encyclopedia. Today most of the content on the Internet is generated by its users, not by the people who build websites. This change in who creates Internet content is the hallmark of Web 2.0.

In Web 2.0 the Internet user is both the consumer of content and the creator of it. Experts describe this as a many-to-many communication model—billions of Internet users creating content and sharing it with billions of others. Control of Internet content is no longer in the hands of a few website builders. It is in the hands of many millions of users.

Web 2.0 differs from Web 1.0 in another important way: The majority of the content is dynamic, not static. The content on

Web 2.0 differs from its predecessor, Web 1.0, in that most online content is generated by its users rather than by website developers. For example, millions of people around the world share information via weblogs, or blogs, like the one pictured here.

social networking websites is always changing, because users update their pages regularly, posting new words, photos, and videos. The new content is sent, or pushed, to the pages of other users in a steady stream, or feed.

To view the new content, the Internet user often does not have to reload, or refresh, the page. The web servers send the new content as soon as it is posted. If a user is online, the new content flows straight into the page in a process known as synchronous communication. If the user is not online, the program saves the content for later viewing, a process known as asynchronous communication. The website might send a short message, known as a push notification, or an alert, to the user, letting him or her know that new content has been added to his or her feed.

Social networking pages are interactive. Users can not only view the content, they can also respond to it. They can rate the content, using an ideogram known as an emoji (such as a smiley face) or other symbol, or write a comment about it. These ratings and comments are pushed to everyone following the same feeds.

Who Invented the Internet?

Today's Internet started out as a small network of interconnected computers called ARPANET. The network was the brainchild of J.C.R. Licklider, Ivan Sutherland, Bob Taylor, and Lawrence G. Roberts, four scientists working at the Advanced Research Projects Agency (ARPA), an agency of the US government. In 1960 Licklider wrote a paper entitled *Man-Computer Symbiosis* that proposed building a network of computers "connected to one another by wide-band communication lines and to individual users by leased-wire services." Licklider enlarged on this idea in a series of memos he wrote while serving as director of Behavioral Sciences and Command and Control Research at ARPA. He left the agency in 1964, but his successors continued to work on the network, which they called ARPANET.

Electronics contractor BBN Technologies began building ARPANET in April 1969. Five months later, computers at the University of California–Los Angeles (UCLA) and Stanford Research Institute (SRI) were connected. On October 29, 1969, UCLA student Charley Kline sent the first message over ARPANET to the computer at SRI.

In December 1969 computers at University of California–Santa Barbara and the University of Utah were added to the network. By December 1970 the network linked thirteen locations, or nodes, of the network, some of which included more than one connected computer. By September 1973 the number of nodes had grown to forty. That year a cable was laid under the Atlantic Ocean to connect to similar networks in Europe. These linked networks grew into the Internet.

J.C.R. Licklider, "Man-Computer Symbiosis," *IRE Transactions on Human Factors in Electronics*, March 1960. http://groups.csail.mit.edu.

Those users, in turn, might respond with a comment of their own. Any number of people can add comments, creating an online conversation. In addition, users can chat with each other using instant messaging windows incorporated into the websites.

User-generated web content does have its critics. They point out that since no one oversees or approves the content that is posted online, it might be—and sometimes is—untrue. For example, someone might share a home remedy for an illness with other people in his or her network, not knowing that scientists have tested the remedy and found it ineffective. A friend reading the post might try the home remedy rather than seeing a doctor or taking a medication that works. As a result, he or she would not get better and could get even worse. Incorrect information about a disease spread over the Internet could pose a public health crisis.

The same is true about faulty financial information, diet advice, travel warnings, and weather predictions. Most social networking websites have software filters that prevent certain kinds of content, such as hate speech and nudity, from being posted, but false information cannot be detected and stopped.

Web 3.0

Just as Web 2.0 grew out of the chat rooms of Web 1.0, so too will Web 3.0 grow out of the real-time notifications and alerts of Web 2.0. The difference will be that in Web 3.0, machines, not human beings, will respond to the alerts.

For example, an Internet user today might become interested in the American film actor Humphrey Bogart after watching a documentary about him. She can go to cable television channel websites and set up e-mail alerts to let her know when movies starring Bogart will be broadcast. When she receives an alert, she can set her digital video recorder (DVR) to record the program. Once the movie has been saved, she can watch it at a convenient time, a process known as time shifting. She might add a note to her electronic calendar to remind her to watch the program.

command

A directive to a computer program to perform a specific task.

In Web 3.0 this user will be able to follow Bogart movies more easily because machines will do more of the work. Rather than signing up for e-mail alerts, she will simply tell her IPA that she wants to watch Bogart movies. The IPA will monitor all the cable channel calendars. When a Bogart movie airs, the IPA will

From Theory to Application

When J.C.R. Licklider proposed building a network of interconnected computers in 1960, his theory required three things: two remote computers and a connection between them. At the time of his writing, many computers existed. What was needed was a way to connect them across distances.

A network of telephone wires already existed. These lines carried not only voice signals, but also data signals for teletype and telephotography (wire photo) machines. The problem was that telephone lines used circuit switching, a method that dedicated one line to each communication session. One computer could connect to several others, but each connection required a separate line.

In 1961 Leonard Kleinrock published a theory for message switching, which would allow many computers to send complete messages over a single line. Two scientists—Paul Baran at Rand Corporation in the United States and Donald Davies at the National Physical Laboratory in the United Kingdom—independently came up with the idea of breaking Kleinrock's complete messages into smaller units. Baran called his units "message blocks" and Davies called his "packets." Both message blocks and packets would be sent to a computer known as an Interface Message Processor, which would store and forward the messages to the receiving computer. The telephone line would never be busy, as dedicated lines often were, because it was in use only when the message block or packet was sent, which took very little time. This process, which became known as packet switching, made the early Internet possible.

compare the title to previous movies that the user has recorded and watched. If she has not seen the movie before, the IPA will set the DVR—which is also connected to the Internet—to record the movie. When the user comes home, she might ask her television, "What did you record?" Her television, like many now on the market, will respond to her voice command. It will display all the new programs that have been time shifted, including the newly recorded Bogart film.

The automatic recording of the Bogart movie is an example of a pervasive web experience. The desired movie would be available for viewing when the user wants it, and machines did nearly all the work, following a machine-to-machine communication model.

The Internet of Things

In this example, the user's television and DVR are part of what is known as the Internet of Things, a network of everyday objects connected to the Internet. Many of these Internet-enabled gadgets exist today. For example, some specially designed homes, known as smarthomes, are equipped with appliances and sensors that can gather and send data over the Internet. These devices include water, electricity, and gas meters; lighting systems; air-conditioning and heating units; refrigerators; and ovens.

Controlled by a central computer and the user's smartphone, the appliances can turn on and off when needed. If sensors show that a room is too cold, the heating system will be turned on. If a room is too hot, the cooling system will turn on. When a user is nearing the home at night, an app in the user's car or smartphone can turn on some of the lights. In Web 3.0, the user will provide the initial settings for devices in the Internet of Things, and then the machines will take over, communicating with each other and responding to the environment without further input from the user.

The Internet of Things now includes wearables—clothing equipped with sensors that collect biometric and activity data and connect to the Internet via wireless systems. For example, a company named Sensoria makes smart socks that track the user's running speed and rhythm. "Sensoria is a wearable platform that can be integrated seamlessly into apparel and other wearable goods that provides quality biometric and user feedback," says Kobie Fuller, a former sprinter and a venture capitalist. "Wearables will become more and more part of our everyday lives. The health and usage data will help inform us on how we can better live our lives, increase athletic performance and more."[1]

> **packet**
>
> **A small unit of data consisting of control information, including a delivery address, and user information.**

A man examines a product known as a wearable—an article of clothing equipped with sensors that collect biometric and activity data about the wearer and connects wirelessly to the Internet. Such devices can monitor the wearer's heart rate, breathing, perspiration, and other vital signs.

Wearables can monitor heart rate, breathing, perspiration, and other vital signs and send alerts to the user telling him or her to eat, drink water, take a medication, rest, or exercise, depending on the user's medical profile. Wearables can also communicate with other machines in the Internet of Things to change the user's environment, raising or lowering room temperature and lighting a room or turning off the light when the user leaves the area. In the future, a wearable might signal a robot to bring the user water when a skin sensor shows he or she needs it or to bring medication at a prescribed time.

About 5.5 million new gadgets are being connected to the Internet of Things every day, according to the market research firm Gartner. The firm estimates that 6.4 billion devices will be connected to the Internet of Things by the end of 2016. Gartner suggests the number of connected devices will grow to nearly 21 billion by 2020. Working together, the Internet of Things will help create the pervasive computer experiences of Web 3.0.

CHAPTER TWO

Cloud Computing

If the Internet is the technological backbone of Web 3.0, cloud computing, or the cloud, is its brain. The Internet enables packets of data to travel between computing devices, but much of that data is stored and processed in clusters of interconnected computers located around the world, known as the cloud. Many of the apps that run on mobile devices such as smartphones and tablets store data in the cloud, rather than on the devices themselves. Often the software that runs the apps is also located in the cloud. Because the cloud's computers, or servers, are located around the world, users are able to access the data more quickly than they could if the data were stored in a single remote location. The speed and power of cloud computing will make pervasive computing experiences possible.

A Public Utility

The first computers were room-sized machines known as mainframe computers. Mainframes were so costly that only universities, large corporations, and the government could afford them. As a result, few people had access to a computer.

Some computer scientists searched for ways to make computers available to more people. John McCarthy, a computer scientist at the Massachusetts Institute of Technology (MIT), developed a software program that would allow a computer to share its resources among many people, using a process known as time-sharing. In a speech at MIT's centennial celebration in 1961, McCarthy suggested that such a system could be used to give the public access to computing power. "If computers of the kind I have advocated become the computers of the future, then computing may someday be organized as a public utility just as the telephone system is a public utility," he said. "The computer utility could become the basis of a new and important industry."[2]

McCarthy's idea languished for decades as electrical engineers focused on bringing computing to the masses by building smaller computers that businesses and home users could afford. At the 1964 New York World's Fair, Olivetti, an Italian company that made typewriters and adding machines, introduced the Programma 101, the first computer small enough to fit on top of a desk. Other small computers, known as desktop computers, followed. These computers ran their own software and saved their data on storage disks inside the machine, known as the hard drive, or on portable magnetic media such as tape and disks.

time-sharing

The sharing of a computing resource among many users at the same time.

Desktop computers were often connected via an electrical network known as a local area network (LAN), usually within one building, or wide area network (WAN), connecting several locations. These networks linked the desktop computers to more powerful computers that stored large amounts of data and performed tasks that the desktop computers could not.

The Evolution of the Cloud

As the Internet grew, John McCarthy's idea of a computer utility became more practical. George Favaloro, a technology analyst at computer maker Compaq, wrote in a 1996 report that computing services delivered over the Internet might someday replace networks of desktop computers linked to local servers. Favaloro stated that not only would remote computers store data, they would also house the software used by local computers. "Application software is no longer a feature of the hardware—but of the Internet," he wrote. Favaloro referred to software programs running on remote servers as "cloud computing–enabled applications."[3]

Compaq shelved the idea of building a computer utility, but other companies such as Amazon, Microsoft, and IBM pursued it. These companies built clusters of high-speed computers that were connected to each other and to the Internet. These computers shared their processing resources. If the usage of one

Early mainframe computers like the one pictured here were expensive as well as being enormous, making them available mainly to government and educational institutions. Few individuals had access to a computer until the advent of the desktop computer in the early 1960s made personal computing possible.

computer reached its maximum capacity, some of the processing load automatically shifted to another computer—a process known as load balancing. The load might be shared with another computer within the local cluster, or it might shift to a computer in a cluster far away. With load balancing, a large computing task would often be performed by a group of computers functioning as a single unit. The group of connected computers became known as the cloud, and the process of sharing resources among many computers became known as cloud computing.

Just as private companies such as Edison Electric and Bell Telephone provided the equipment and infrastructure for electricity and telephone utilities in the early 1900s, so too did private companies build the "computer utility" in the early 2000s. Amazon introduced the Elastic Compute Cloud, the first cloud Infrastructure as a Service (IaaS), in 2006. Microsoft introduced its Azure IaaS in 2008, and IBM launched its SmartCloud in 2011. These cloud computing platforms were offered to both organizations and individuals who needed new or additional computing power.

Because computers in the cloud share their resources, they are able to handle workload increases quickly—a function known as scalability. For example, when a cloud user has a large increase in data processing needs, the computers in the cloud automatically "scale up" to handle the workload by sharing it across the network. When the workload drops, the cloud computers "scale down."

Like water and electricity utilities, cloud providers charge by usage. Because of the cloud's scalability and its business model, Simon Ponsford, a British cloud computing expert, defines the cloud as "infinitely scalable, shared computing resources available on demand via the Internet where the user is charged only for what he uses."[4]

With the coming of the cloud, computing companies such as Apple, Google, and Microsoft began to offer cloud services not only to businesses but also to individuals. Apple iCloud, Google Drive, and Microsoft OneDrive all allow users to work on, share, and store documents, photos, and videos in the cloud. Not only is the content stored in the cloud, the software used to create the content also resides in the cloud instead of the user's local device. Because cloud providers want to attract and retain users, they offer these services at little or no charge. These cloud providers generally earn revenue by sharing information about their users' accounts and online activities with advertisers. A report by Cisco, a maker of computer networking equipment, states that 1.5 billion Internet users now store at least some of their personal data in the cloud. Cisco expects the number of personal cloud storage users to grow to 2 billion by 2019.

scalability

The capability of a system to handle a growing amount of work.

Companies like Amazon, Apple, and Netflix, which sell digital content such as e-books, music, and movies online, also store their content in the cloud. Their customers can create virtual libraries of their purchases and then download or stream the content as desired. Since music and video files are large, saving them locally consumes a great deal of space on a user's hard drive. By streaming content from the cloud, users save storage space on their computers. The same is true for the users' own video, music, and photo files: By uploading their files to the cloud, users save space on their local device. In addition, with their files stored in the cloud, users can upgrade or change their computer hardware without having to copy files from one device to another. If a user's device stops working, is lost, or is stolen, the files stored in the cloud are not affected.

Mobile Devices and the Cloud

At the same time that the Internet was developing, a revolution was occurring in telephone communications that would affect the Internet as well. Wireless telephones, which received radio signals from cellular towers, became smaller and less expensive than earlier wireless phones. And whereas the previous wireless phones relied on a continuous open radio signal between the two callers, the newer phones sent packets of digital data between the two callers, just as packets of data were sent between computers on the Internet. The speaker's phone converted the electronic signal from the microphone into packets of data and sent them to the listener's phone. The listener's phone converted

Cloud storage services such as Apple's iCloud enable users to store, share, and work on documents, photos, and videos in the cloud, with groups of connected computers functioning as a single unit. Both businesses and individual users employ such services.

iCloud

From Theory to Application

In April 1961 John McCarthy described a new computing model. He believed it would be possible to offer computing services to the public by letting individuals connect to a remote computer, just as they connect to a power grid to receive electricity from a power plant. He called this provisioning model a "computer utility."

McCarthy had recently completed work on one of the key components to make the theory practical. He had written software that allowed many users to access a computer at the same time. This method differed from the existing model, known as batch processing, in which a single user, or operator, would enter computing jobs one at a time.

The next step was to equip users with affordable computers to access the larger computers. Desktop computers were introduced in 1964, but since they could run their own programs, there was little need to connect to a remote computer. In addition, data transmission over existing telephone lines was slow. In the 1980s, however, telephone companies began to install fiber-optic cabling, which was capable of faster data transmission.

By the end of the 1990s, fiber-optic cabling was in place in much of the world. The advent of smartphones, which have relatively little storage capacity, and the growing desire for data-rich content such as videos, rekindled interest in the idea of using remote computers to store data and run applications. In 2006 Amazon introduced the Elastic Compute Cloud, a provisioning service almost identical to McCarthy's computing utility.

the data into an electronic signal that activated a small speaker, reproducing the speaker's voice.

Because the data being sent between phones was digital, cell phones were able to transmit more than voice data. Users could send text messages back and forth, a process that became known as texting. Phone makers began to add small digital cameras to their phones, which allowed users to take digital photographs and even video clips, store them on their phones, and send them to other phones. A giant leap forward came when cell phone makers enabled their phones to connect to the Internet. Web-enabled phones became known as smartphones.

Initially, this advance was created to allow cell phone users to send and receive e-mail, electronic messages sent over the Internet via computer. The ability to check an e-mail inbox and to respond to e-mails using a phone, rather than waiting to use a computer, was a huge convenience. For people in business, in which a quick response to an e-mail could mean the difference between a task getting done on time or not, smartphones became a necessity.

The same technology that allowed smartphone users to connect to e-mail servers over the Internet would also allow them to connect to websites. All that was needed was for the smartphone to be equipped with an Internet browser to translate the data packets into an interactive page on the screen. This occurred in 1996 with the introduction of the Nokia 9000 Communicator, which offered web browsing but displayed only text. Other phone makers soon followed. Within a few years, smartphones were equipped with full-color, fully functional web browsers. Internet users no longer had to connect to the Internet through a cable or wireless router. They could simply open their phones and connect through their cellular network.

With the introduction of the Apple iPhone in 2007 and the Android mobile operating system in 2008, the smartphone universe expanded at an astonishing rate. By 2015, 2.6 billion people had smartphone subscriptions. That number is forecast to grow to 6.1 billion by 2020. In many countries, especially in the developing world, more people connect to the Internet with smartphones than with computers. For example, in India, the world's second-most populous country, 72 percent the nation's Internet traffic is through smartphones. In Nigeria the figure is even higher; 76 percent of Nigeria's web traffic is through smartphones.

Because of their small size, smartphones and other mobile devices such as tablets and phablets (smartphones with large screens) have limited space to store files. As a result, smartphone users often save photos, videos, and documents in the cloud.

Innovative Ideas for Cooling Data Centers

If a server gets too warm, it will power off to prevent damage to its sensitive electronic components. To keep servers running, data centers must be kept cool. Traditional air-conditioning systems consume about half the power data centers use. Now cloud provider Microsoft is looking at keeping data centers cool by placing them undersea.

In 2015 Microsoft deployed an underwater data center prototype—named Leona Philpot, after a character in Microsoft's *Halo* video game series—off the coast of California. The steel capsule was filled with nitrogen gas, which cools more efficiently than air does, and was outfitted with heat exchangers that used the ocean's cold water to cool the gas. Submerged in 30 feet (9 m) of water, the data center ran for 105 days without overheating. Microsoft is now building a prototype that will be three times larger and will capture the energy of moving seawater to power the unit.

Three years before Microsoft's undersea experiment, cloud computing expert Simon Ponsford submitted a similar plan to the government of Qatar. Ponsford proposed placing a data center in a sealed container near the Persian Gulf coast. Instead of filling the container with gas, Ponsford planned to immerse the servers in pharmaceutical grade oil, also known as baby oil, which does not conduct electricity well or ignite easily. The oil would be pumped to a heat exchanger 30 feet (9 m) underwater, 200 yards (183 m) off the coast. Ponsford estimated the oil-based cooling system would use twenty-five times less energy than traditional systems do. Ponsford believes the success of Leona Philpot might rekindle interest in his plan.

The software that powers many smartphone apps also resides in the cloud, not on the local device. "When you pull out your smartphone you think you're using this miraculous little computer, but actually you're using more than 100 computers out in this thing called the cloud,"[5] explains Peter Lee, corporate vice president for Microsoft Research.

For example, some of the software for the music discovery

app Shazam resides in a user's smartphone, but more of it resides in the cloud. When the user wants to identify a song that is playing nearby, the app in the smartphone converts the tune received through the microphone into digital packets and sends them to the cloud. The software running in the cloud performs the larger task of comparing the tune to the thousands of songs stored in a database located in the cloud. If the software finds a match, it sends the title of the song back to the user's device. The user might think his or her smartphone identified the song, but most of the work was performed by servers in the cloud.

Thin Clients

The ability to access cloud-based databases and run powerful software from smartphones has led some experts to wonder whether mobile devices will replace desktop and laptop computers. In a 2016 *Wired* magazine article, Christina Bonnington wrote, "We're at the point where anyone armed with a current model smartphone or tablet is able to handle almost all of their at-home—and even at-work—tasks without needing anything else. We're living proof: for the last two years, *WIRED* has been able to cover events like CES [Consumer Electronics Show] almost exclusively using our smartphones."[6]

Carolina Milanesi, chief of research and head of US business at Kantar Worldpanel ComTech, a global market research firm that studies technology trends, agrees. "Will we always need a desktop? No, not all of us will," says Milanesi. "Some of us already don't."[7] Milanesi thinks this is especially true in the developing world. She says:

> In emerging markets, many consumers experienced the Internet, e-mail, and apps through a phone first, and the transition from that to a tablet or a phablet is natural. As processing power continues to improve and prices continue to decrease, we could see consumers use these devices to power external screens. Certainly many users will not walk the path that many of us in mature markets walked.[8]

Thousands of businesses already use small, fast computers connected to monitors and keyboards to run applications that reside in the cloud. These computers are known as thin clients. For example, British computer maker Cranberry sells a thin client that is about the size of a paperback book. The Cranberry computer has a very fast processor and a large external bus, the communication system that transfers data between a computer and other devices. Together these components allow the Cranberry computer to send and receive large amounts of data over the Internet at very high speed. Like a smartphone or a tablet, the Cranberry computer has no internal hard drive or moving parts of any kind. However, it has enough random access memory to perform basic tasks, such as running an Internet browser. Unlike a smartphone, the Cranberry computer has several external ports for connecting to a keyboard, monitor, printer, and other devices.

> **thin client**
>
> **A small, lightweight computer with limited storage capability designed to interact with a remote server, which performs most computing functions.**

Software as a Service (SaaS) companies offer software that resides in the cloud and can be accessed by thin clients. This software is called a hosted desktop. The software creates an image on the user's screen that looks exactly like the desktop of a PC or laptop, with taskbars and software icons in the usual places. When the hosted desktop user performs a task such as opening a spreadsheet or word-processing document, the thin client sends the command to a server in the cloud. The software in the cloud then opens a file and sends the new image to the thin client.

Latency

When a person uses a hosted desktop, the local computing device sends packets of data to the cloud each time the user presses the keyboard to type a letter. The software in the cloud places the letter into a virtual document and sends the image back to the user. It takes time for the packets of data to travel from the user's device to the cloud and back, creating a brief delay during typing.

Software as a Service (SaaS) companies offer what is called a hosted desktop, which creates an image on the user's screen that looks exactly like the typical desktop of a PC or laptop. The software accessible through this desktop, however, is stored in the cloud rather than on the user's device.

The delay between a keystroke and seeing the letter or number appear on the screen is called latency. Because both the thin client and the cloud-based servers have fast Internet connections, the user usually cannot tell that the work is being done on a remote computer. Even when the user is typing, the latency period is so short that the user is unaware that the document is being created in the cloud.

Hosted desktops offer many benefits to businesses. For example, the software running the hosted desktop is kept up-to-date by the SaaS provider. As a result, the company using the hosted desktop does not have to buy or install expensive software upgrades. The company also does not have to buy new servers for data storage. All the content created on the hosted desktop is stored in the cloud, which has unlimited storage. Most computer maintenance is performed by the SaaS provider as well, reducing the need for support staff at the local level. Since the data is stored in the cloud, the hosted desktops are immune to local disasters. If a fire, flood, earthquake, or other disaster destroys a company's thin clients, the stored data remains intact in the cloud, ready to be accessed by new thin clients. Because of these advantages, many experts believe cloud-connected thin clients will replace PCs and laptops in the business world in the next few years.

The cloud-based hosted desktop model is almost exactly what John McCarthy had in mind when he described a computer utility that would provide software and storage from a remote location on a pay-as-you-go basis. Cisco estimates that by 2019, 86 percent of computing workloads will be processed in the cloud, while only 14 percent will be processed by traditional data centers. By allowing users to store and access vast amounts of data quickly from anywhere in the world, the cloud provides the physical foundation for Web 3.0 and pervasive computing experiences.

CHAPTER THREE

Big Data

Each day millions of Internet users around the world share pictures, videos, and written updates on social media platforms, creating vast amounts of Internet content. Since this content is digital, computers can be used to analyze it. However, some collections of this data, known as data sets, are so large and complex that traditional software cannot process them within a useful time. Such data sets are known as big data. Computer scientists are developing new algorithms to make sense of big data.

Big data can be useful in many ways. For example, by analyzing the location and content of social media posts during and after a natural disaster, authorities can pinpoint the worst damage, allowing them to target relief efforts quickly. The same is true for the outbreak of a disease: Researchers can track posts and tweets to see how the disease is spreading. This data can sometimes reveal where the disease originated and predict where the next outbreaks might be.

Using a practice known as customer relationship management, some businesses mine big data to build customer loyalty and attract new customers. For example, a company might enter into an agreement with Facebook or Twitter to receive information about users' profiles, likes, and posts. The company then combines this data with its own customer information and perhaps other data, such as records from the company's suppliers, vendors, and distributors. These data sets often are so large that the company will engage a cloud-based software service provider such as Salesforce, Microsoft, SAP, or Oracle to analyze the big data for them. The SaaS providers mine the big data to identify potential new customers and the most loyal existing customers so the company can target them with ads and special offers.

Sources of Big Data

Social networking websites such as Facebook, Twitter, Instagram, Tumblr, Snapchat, and YouTube generate huge amounts of data. Twitter users post an average of 6,000 tweets every second, which adds up to 500 million tweets per day. Instagram users upload an average of 487 pictures every second, or more than 42 million photos a day. YouTube users upload an average of 300 hours' worth of video every minute, or 432,000 hours of video per day. YouTube users view 4 billion videos per day, while Facebook users watch 100 million hours of video a day. Since video files are much larger than text messages and even photographs, the uploading, sharing, and streaming of videos constitutes 75 percent of all Internet traffic.

Not all big data is generated by humans. Wireless sensors that monitor water, oil, and gas pipelines; power lines; streets; and highways also produce large amounts of data. Surveillance cameras located in and around businesses and public buildings, at intersections, on bridges, and elsewhere collect vast amounts of visual data. Sensors in gadgets of the Internet of Things are already generating data, and they likely will produce more as they become more popular. International Data Corporation, a provider of market intelligence, estimates that by 2020 fully 10 percent of the world's data will be generated by the Internet of Things, up from just 2 percent in 2014. According to the corporation, the Internet of Things will produce 4.4 zettabytes of data—enough to fill a stack of iPads reaching two-thirds of the way to the moon.

> **algorithm**
>
> A set of steps or operations that are followed in order to solve a mathematical problem or to complete a computer process.

Scientific research, too, generates enormous amounts of data. For example, the *Rosetta* space probe and its robotic lander, *Philae*, which are exploring the comet 67P/Churyumov-Gerasimenko, have sent thousands of digital images back to Earth. These high-resolution pictures have created huge data sets that are available to scientists on the Internet. The same is true for the *Cassini-Huygens* spacecraft, which has been orbiting the planet Saturn since 2004. The Hubble Space Telescope, which has been orbiting the earth since 1990, has made 1.2 million observations and

The uploading, sharing, and streaming of videos constitutes 75 percent of all Internet traffic. Users of Facebook alone watch 100 million hours of video every day.

has generated 100 terabytes of data. The telescope now adds 10 terabytes of data to its archive every year.

Another source of vast amounts of data is biomedical research. In 2003 scientists working on the Human Genome Project completed the mapping of the 3.3 billion chemical units in the human genetic instruction set. This data is available on the Internet to scientists around the world who are seeking to find causes of diseases and ways to treat them using a process known as genomics. In this research, scientists use computers to compare sections of the human genome taken from both healthy and diseased volunteers to see if they can identify the genetic differences that cause a disease. They also study the genomes from populations that are known to have high levels of a certain disease, such as cancer or diabetes, to see if they can find which genes increase the chances of getting the disease. Such studies require and generate big data.

In 2016 a team of scientists

zettabyte

One sextillion (1,000,000,000,000,000,000,000) bytes, or 10^{21} bytes.

analyzed the complete genomic information of 1,122 patients with brain cancer to see if they could find a reason why some patients who are diagnosed with slow-growing tumors die from the disease quickly, while others with faster-growing tumors are able to survive for several years. The study, published in the biology journal *Cell*, focused on molecular features of gliomas, the most common type of brain tumor, and suggested ways to better treat patients. According to Michele Ceccarelli, a senior scientist at Hamad bin Khalifa University in Doha, Qatar, and lead author of the study:

> **natural language processing**
>
> **The ability of a computer program to understand human speech as it is spoken.**

This project is an example of the advantage of Big Data. . . . In order to make our discovery, we worked with a network of more than 300 scientists from around the world. We analyzed the millions of pieces of information that formed a "data tsunami" in order to identify common characteristics of various groups of glioma. As a result of our analysis we discovered two novel subgroups of patients that were previously unknown.[9]

Analyzing Big Data

Computer scientists are developing new tools to analyze the content generated in social media to make big data useful, including natural language processing and sentiment analysis. These emerging technologies will play an even larger role in Web 3.0.

To a computer, words posted online are just strings of digits, devoid of meaning, until the computer is programmed with a dictionary. Even then, a single word can mean many things, depending on how it is used. The computer must learn these different meanings. In addition, the meaning of a sentence in English depends on the order of the words, or syntax. The sentence "The boy ate the chocolate bar" means something very different from "The chocolate bar ate the boy," even though both sentences use

These images of the Whirlpool Galaxy were transmitted to Earth from the Hubble Space Telescope. Since entering orbit in 1990, the telescope has generated 100 terabytes of data and continues to add 10 terabytes a year to this total.

the same words. Computers must be taught rules for deciding the meanings of strings of words.

Preslav Nakov, a senior scientist at Qatar Computing Research Institute, points out, "Machines are still a long way from understanding everyday speech the way the computer Hal does in the motion picture *2001: A Space Odyssey*."[10] Nakov and his collaborator, Marti Hearst, a professor at the University of California–Berkeley, have developed software to help solve the problem of compound modifiers in English. For example, the meaning of the phrase "plastic water bottle" is clear to a human being, but a computer finds this phrase difficult to understand. The machine does not know whether it refers to a water bottle made of plastic or a bottle containing something called "plastic water."

A World Record for Tweets

The social media website Twitter is one of the most popular sources of big data for researchers interested in testing sentiment analysis algorithms. The first tweet was sent on March 21, 2006, by Jack Dorsey, the creator of Twitter. It took more than three years for the number of tweets to reach 1 billion. Today it takes less than two days for 1 billion tweets to be sent.

Twitter users often mark their tweets with a hashtag (#) to identify the topic of the tweet. Sometimes people use a popular hashtag to show solidarity with a person, cause, entertainment program, or sports team. Tweets with the same hashtag can be viewed in the Twitter feed by interested readers. The most popular hashtags are shown in a trending box on the website.

On October 24, 2015, Twitter users following an episode of a popular television show featuring Alden Richards and Maine "Yaya Dub" Mendoza in the Philippines posted more than 41 million tweets in one day using the hashtag #ALDubEBTamanPanahon—a world record for most tweets in a twenty-four-hour period using a single hashtag. The burst of tweets broke the record of 35.6 million tweets sent during the World Cup semifinal match played between Brazil and Germany on July 8, 2014. At one point during the episode, which aired live from the Philippine Arena, fans sent more than forty-eight thousand tweets per minute as Richards sang the couple's theme song to Mendoza.

Creating a program so a computer will understand complex phrases such as compound modifiers that it encounters when analyzing big data is a challenging task. For example, people sometimes use surface markers such as hyphens when creating compound modifiers. The computer must be taught what to do when it finds a surface marker. Sometimes the hyphen will appear between the first and second words, as in "cell-cycle analysis," and sometimes it will appear between the second and third words, as in "tumor cell-cycle." The software must have rules to handle these situations. The same is true when writers use parentheses, as in "(cell cycle) analysis," or slash marks between words, as in "cell/cycle analysis."

To test their natural language processing algorithms, Nakov and Hearst used Internet search engines such as Google, Bing, and Yahoo! to see how often certain phrases, such as "analysis of the cell cycle" and "cell-cycle analysis," appeared in content on the Internet. They then used these statistics to refine their algorithms. "Creating a successful algorithm requires real-world knowledge, which has proven very hard to collect and make available to computers to use," explained Nakov. "To give a computer such real-world knowledge on the fly and to solve the problem, we collected various statistics from the largest available text corpus in the world: the Web."[11] Using these results, Nakov and Hearst were able to create a software program capable of understanding the syntax and semantics of compound modifiers in English. This was a small but important step forward for a number of natural language processing applications such as machine translation, question answering, and information retrieval that will help computers understand human speech and enable them to create pervasive computing experiences in Web 3.0.

> **sentiment analysis**
>
> **Using a software program to analyze text to determine the writer's attitude toward a particular topic.**

Sentiment Analysis

Words posted online convey not only meaning but also emotion. Scientists working in the research field known as sentiment analysis write programs designed to detect the feelings expressed in big data. Algorithms for sentiment analysis are also complex. Not only must the program search for words that convey emotions, such as "love" and "hate," but also words written in happiness or anger, such as "brilliant" or "stupid." Punctuation must also be considered. For example, "brilliant!!!" might carry greater emotional weight than "brilliant" or even "brilliant!" Capital letters, such as "BRILLIANT," emoticons, and emojis also indicate feelings.

The Four Vs of Big Data

Some computing experts describe big data as being characterized by four Vs: volume, variety, velocity, and veracity. For big data to be useful, computer scientists must devise algorithms that address all four Vs of big data.

Volume—the amount of data—is the characteristic that gives big data its name. To be considered big data, the volume must exceed the capability of a user to process it using traditional data processing software.

Variety refers to the fact that big data is made up of unstructured data. Data comes in two forms: structured and unstructured. Structured data refers to data of one type. For example, the data processed by financial software typically would be numerals followed by two decimal places, corresponding to money. Unstructured data could be numerals, text, photographs, video files—anything.

Velocity refers to the frequency of incoming data to be processed. Big data often consists of streaming data from online sources such as social media posts.

Veracity refers to the accuracy of data. Not all data is accurate, or "clean." Big data typically is made up of both accurate and inaccurate data.

Some figures of speech are difficult for a machine to understand. Sarcasm—saying one thing but meaning the opposite—is hard for a machine to detect. "The prime minister is sooooooo smart" could mean that the person posting the comment believes the prime minister is highly intelligent. However, it could also mean the prime minister is not intelligent at all. The sentiment analysis program must have rules to recognize sarcasm.

The best way to determine if a sentiment analysis tool is working well is to test its findings against human results. For example, a researcher might use a sentiment analysis tool to rate a series of statements for their emotional content and then have a group of people rate the same statements. The human ratings often are done by large groups of people working together on the Internet, a technique known as crowdsourcing. If the sentiment analysis tool's ratings are close to the human ratings—80 percent accuracy or better—the tool is considered a success.

Sentiment analysis can be used to analyze the popularity of products, companies, social causes, and even political candidates. For example, during the 2015 elections for Parliament in the United Kingdom, SaaS provider Tivarri allowed the public free access to a sentiment analysis tool called Brandango to track the emotional content of comments being made on Twitter about candidates from seven political parties.

Unlike a poll, which samples the opinions of a small number of people, Brandango analyzed all relevant tweets. Normally it takes days or even weeks to collect and analyze big data, but Brandango was able to process millions of incoming tweets rapidly enough to produce new reports every fifteen minutes, viewable as a changing chart. The election algorithm did not treat all tweets the same way. It gave greater weight to tweets from people with a higher number of followers, reasoning that these comments reached more people and had more influence. The tool was also able to detect organized efforts to influence social media, a practice known as "astroturfing," and discount these tweets. The result was a highly accurate, graphical depiction of the changing sentiments of millions of UK voters.

Artificial Intelligence for Disaster Response

Big data has been combined with natural language processing, sentiment analysis, and other technologies to help direct relief efforts when natural disasters have struck. These efforts have shown the potential of big data, but they have also revealed the current limits of computer-based reasoning, also known as artificial intelligence.

On April 25, 2015, an earthquake measuring 7.8 on the Richter scale (or 8.1, according to Chinese authorities) struck the mountainous nation of Nepal about 40 miles (64 km) from the capital of Kathmandu, killing more than eight thousand people and injuring more than twenty-one thousand. Officials at the United Nations (UN) reached out to Patrick Meier, cofounder of

Survivors search through rubble after the devastating April 25, 2015, earthquake that struck the nation of Nepal. Analyzing social media posts in the aftermath of the quake enabled rescue workers to quickly assess in which areas aid would be most needed.

the Harvard Humanitarian Initiative's Program on Crisis Mapping and Early Warning at Harvard University. Meier, along with an international team of scientists and programmers, had developed the Artificial Intelligence for Disaster Response (AIDR) platform, a software program that collects, identifies, and classifies social media messages posted after a natural disaster.

Because lives are at stake in such a situation, Meier and his team also use a second platform, MicroMappers, to analyze social media content. MicroMappers does not rely on artificial intelligence alone. Instead, it uses crowdsourcing to assess and classify the messages online. After the earthquake in Nepal, twenty-eight hundred human volunteers reviewed more than three hundred thousand tweets collected by AIDR. The volunteers placed each tweet into one of four categories: request for help, casualty figure or infrastructure damage update, offer of help, or none of the above.

Based on these human assessments, the MicroMappers software plotted the locations of the most urgent tweets on crisis maps. Meier and his team sent the maps via the Internet to relief agencies so they could focus on the areas requiring immediate attention. "Within 24 hours of the first tremors in Nepal, the UN [was] asking us to initiate AIDR and MicroMappers," explained Meier. "This early activation meant we had the opportunity to put together live crisis maps of the most affected areas and then feed these to several relief agencies before they had even arrived in Nepal. This meant that responders had a good picture of the areas that had received the worst of the damage before they had even touched down in Kathmandu."[12]

Meier and his team of digital humanitarians are credited with saving lives in the wake of the Nepal earthquake, but their involvement shows the limits of artificial intelligence when handling big data: Human beings were still needed to assess the data. That is not the end of the story, however. The MicroMappers assessments are being used to "train" AIDR to better classify tweets based on their urgency. The goal is to have machines that can interpret incoming big data and dispatch relief efforts more quickly and more accurately than human beings can, saving even more lives.

As the number of Internet users grows and the number of devices in the Internet of Things increases, more real-world data will be generated from more places than ever before. This data—big data—has the potential to improve the quality of life by providing a more accurate picture of events as they unfold, from natural disasters and pandemics to traffic jams and changing weather. Big data can smooth out the rough edges of unpredictability and create a more efficient society and better life for humankind, but only if it is processed and applied quickly. Devising the algorithms that will enable machines to use big data is one of the greatest challenges of creating Web 3.0.

CHAPTER FOUR

The Semantic Web

The Internet connects 75 million servers worldwide that store at least 13 billion web pages. Many of these web servers share their resources in the cloud. Nevertheless, the pages for each website are stored in separate databases in what are sometimes called data silos.

Internet users can search through these data silos using a search engine such as Google, Bing, or Yahoo!, but search engines look only for pages that contain the term or terms entered by the user. For example, if an Internet user searches the term "Shakespeare," the search engine will provide links to pages that contain that word. Some pages might be about the English playwright William Shakespeare; some might feature Shakespeare brand fishing rods; some might discuss Shakespeare and Company bookstores and cafes. Search engines rank the pages using a complex formula that puts the most relevant pages at the top, but they do not use artificial intelligence to analyze the data. The Internet user must read through the search engine results to decide which pages contain the information he or she is looking for. Today's Internet is "a place where computers do the presentation (easy) and people do the linking and interpreting (hard),"[13] writes Alexandra I. Cristea, an associate professor at University of Warwick in Coventry, England.

Some Internet experts, such as Tim Berners-Lee, would like to see this situation change. Berners-Lee is the Nobel Prize-winning computer scientist who developed the World Wide Web, the information system that identifies documents and other resources by URLs and connects them with links so they can be accessed via the Internet. Berners-Lee envisions the Internet functioning as a single, unified database rather than as a collection of billions of web pages. Such a resource would be enormous—so big that, like other big data, it could be processed only by computers running specialized programs. In his 1999 book *Weaving the Web*, Berners-Lee referred to this resource as the semantic web:

I have a dream for the Web . . . and it has two parts. In the first part, the Web becomes a much more powerful means for collaboration between people. . . . In the second part of the dream, collaborations extend to computers. Machines become capable of analyzing all of the data on the Web—the content, links, and transactions between people and computers. A "Semantic Web," which should make this possible, has yet to emerge, but when it does, the day-to-day mechanisms of trade, bureaucracy, and our daily lives will be handled by machines talking to machines, leaving humans to provide the inspiration and intuition.[14]

The problem today is that machines cannot make sense of much of the data on web pages created in Web 2.0. Current web pages lack the metadata—data that describes other data—that would allow machines to interact with the content. "Most of the Web's content today is designed for humans to read, not for computer programs to manipulate meaningfully,"[15] writes Berners-Lee. To make the dream of a semantic web a reality, Berners-Lee is leading an effort to add metadata to new and existing web pages. This metadata will allow machines to browse the Internet and interpret the data without human assistance.

metadata

Data that provides information about other data to increase its usefulness.

Berners-Lee created the semantic web initiative as an extension of the work of the World Wide Web Consortium (W3C), the international organization that he founded in 1994 to establish technical standards for the World Wide Web. W3C has created procedures for marking up web pages with tags that can be read and used by software programs. These machine-readable tags are known as semantic notation. So far, website builders working with W3C standards have added the semantic notation to about 4 million websites.

One kind of semantic notation is known as the Resource Description Framework (RDF). This form of semantic notation was designed to help machines understand the relationships between

An Internet search today using the term "Shakespeare" might yield websites about the famous English playwright (pictured) or about completely unrelated topics, because such searches produce results based only on the appearance of the search term on a page. In the future, artificial intelligence may be employed to go a step further and analyze the context surrounding the search term, leading to results more targeted to the user's interests.

words on a web page. RDF works by connecting two words in a way that makes sense to a machine. One word is known as a subject, and the other word is known as an object. To help the machine understand how these words are related, a third word, known as a predicate, is used to link them. For example, a website might say, "Shakespeare wrote *Macbeth*." RDF would treat "Shakespeare" as the subject, "wrote" as the predicate, and "*Macbeth*" as the object. By placing each word into one of three categories—subject, predicate, or object—RDF allows a machine to understand the relationships between the words in the same way that a human reader does. The categories tell the machine that something known as a "Shakespeare" acted upon

Markup Language

While working at the European Organization for Nuclear Research in 1989, British physicist Tim Berners-Lee proposed that the laboratory adopt an Internet-based communication system using hypertext—text displayed on a computer screen with digital links to other text. Berners-Lee wrote specifications for the language, which he called hypertext markup language (HTML), as well as software to display the language, called a browser. HTML became the foundation of the World Wide Web.

HTML uses tags written with angle brackets (< >) to provide information about text on the page. Tags surrounding words tell a browser how to display or link the text. For example, the tags <i> and </i> tell the browser that the word between them should appear in italics. Browsers do not display the tags; they only interpret them. The tagged word <i>Macbeth</i> would appear as *Macbeth*.

HTML tells machines how to display content, but not what the content means. Berners-Lee realized that a new markup language was needed to allow machines to understand relationships between words on a page and also between the words and other words on the web. This could be accomplished by putting identifying terms and links within angle brackets. For example, the statement "William Shakespeare was born in Stratford-on-Avon" might appear as:

```
<div vocab="http://schema.org/" typeof="Person">
<span property="name">William Shakespeare</span> was born in
<span property="birthPlace" typeof="Place" href="http://www.
wikidata.org/entity/Q189288">
<span property="name">Stratford-on-Avon</span>.
</span>
</div>
```

Like HTML, the markups within brackets, known as semantic web notation, are not displayed to human readers but can be understood by machines.

something known as a "Macbeth." Thanks to RDF, the machine does not think that something known as a *Macbeth* acted upon something known as a "Shakespeare." Because RDF always requires three elements, each RDF notation is known as a "triple."

To help the machine understand what a "Shakespeare" is and what a *Macbeth* is, RDF also provides a way for the words to be linked to online resources that define the terms. For example, hyperlinks attached to "Shakespeare" and *Macbeth* might point to the DBPedia database, which describes 4.58 million things, including 1,445,000 persons, 735,000 places, and 411,000 creative works. The DBPedia definitions will help a software application such as an intelligent personal assistant (IPA) better understand the words on a web page.

Another form of metadata, RDF Schema (RDFS), builds on the RDF information to further classify the data for machines. For example, RDFS would classify "Shakespeare" not only as a subject, but also as a person. Likewise, it would classify *Macbeth* not only as an object, but also as a play. Other metadata can point to where Shakespeare was born, how long he lived, what he wrote, and other facts. By linking data about people, places, and things across the Internet, semantic notation will allow machines to access all the online information about a specific topic at one time, rather than having to search through individual web pages. Data will no longer be housed in silos; it will be connected in an ever-growing, ever-changing web—"a Web of data rather than a Web of documents,"[16] as Berners-Lee puts it.

> **ontology**
>
> In computer science, a formal naming and definition of the types, properties, and interrelationships of the various entities.

Making web pages machine readable and linking their data is only the beginning of the process, however. The semantic web also needs a system that allows machines to reason with the linked data. W3C has embraced another markup system known as Web Ontology Language that allows computers to bring together data from many online sources and infer new knowledge based on existing knowledge. For example, a machine might learn that John Shakespeare was the father of William Shakespeare. It might also know that a father is a subclass of parent. From these two facts, the machine can infer that John Shakespeare was a parent of William Shakespeare. Although this inference might not seem brilliant, a computer is capable of performing thousands of such operations per second, allowing the machine to draw intelligent conclusions. Using such brute force logic, the IBM computer Watson was able to defeat Ken Jennings and Brad Rutter, the two most successful champions of the television game show *Jeopardy!*, in a special three-day tournament of the popular game show. The ability of a machine to make intelligent inferences is the foundation of Web 3.0.

The Semantic Web at Work

One of the most successful uses of semantic web technology to date was deployed at the British Broadcasting Corporation (BBC), the largest broadcasting corporation in the world. The BBC, which operates eight national television channels, ten national radio channels, and forty local radio stations, posts a great deal of content to its website in the form of text, audio, and video. As a public service broadcaster, the BBC has a mission to make its content easily available to the public. The BBC formerly used separate, standalone website domains, or microsites, to promote individual programs such as *Top Gear* and content regarding certain special interests such as news, cooking, and gardening. However, BBC executives believed these websites fell short of the organization's goal of making its content easy to access:

microsites

An individual web page or a small group of pages within an existing website often dedicated to a single topic and having a unique domain name.

> These sites can be very successful, but tend not to link together, and so are less useful when people have interests that span program brands or domains. For example, we

The BBC launched an initiative in 2007 to use semantic web notation to link its programs with each other and with outside resources, enabling, for example, fans of the television series Top Gear *(pictured, with hosts James May, Richard Hammond, and Jeremy Clarkson), to locate other online content matched to their individual interests.*

can tell you who presents Top Gear, but not what else those people have presented. As a user it is very difficult to find everything the BBC has published about any given subject, nor can you easily navigate across BBC domains.[17]

Another problem was that the BBC's websites showcased only a small amount of the network's programming. "As the BBC broadcasts between 1,000 and 1,500 programs a day, the long tail of our programming didn't get any web presence," stated the executives. The BBC offered feeds of its content to other websites, but these feeds also lacked usefulness, according to BBC executives. They wrote, "These feeds suffer from the same or similar issues to the microsites; namely they lack interlinking. That is, it is possible to get a feed of latest news stories but it's not easy to segment that data into news stories about 'Lions'. Nor is it possible to query the data to extract the specific data required."[18]

To put more of its content on the Internet in a useful form, the BBC launched an initiative in 2007 to use semantic web notation

The Semantic Web and Censorship

Some advocates of free expression have raised concerns about the semantic web. They fear that the machine-readable markup language will make it easier for governments to use computers to locate, target, and block objectionable content. Julien Mailland, an assistant professor at Indiana University, believes that the semantic web's meta-tagging can be misused. "Allowing meta-tags of information to be a crucial tool of retrieval of information in the Internet age is equivalent to allowing a meta-authority to classify—and to exclude—information on our behalf," he says. "While the Internet allowed the populace to break away from such shackles, the semantic web could lead us backwards."

Mailland argues that content-blocking software filters have not been widely used because they often block harmless material in a process known as spillover. Mailland points out that the semantic web will allow filters to be much more accurate, because the machines will understand the context of the pages. This increased accuracy could mean that the use of software filters will grow. Mailland writes:

> What has so far protected citizens eager to access information freely from filtering and censorship schemes was in part the fact that such systems involved so many spillover effects that censors were, in certain countries and to a certain extent, reluctant to adopt them on a large scale. Ironically though, the creation of more subtle filtering and labeling tools with less spillover effect might lead to more censorship.

Julien Mailland, "The Semantic Web and Information Flow: A Legal Framework," *North Carolina Journal of Law & Technology*, Spring 2010, pp. 271, 281–82.

to link its programs with each other and with outside resources. For example, the BBC Wildlife Finder now provides a semantic web identifier for every species covered on the BBC. Meanwhile, BBC Nature links to data from different sources, including *Wikipedia*, the World Wildlife Fund's Wildfinder, the International Union for

Conservation of Nature's Red List of Threatened Species, the Zoological Society of London's EDGE of Existence program, and the Animal Diversity Web. All these outside resources are also linked through semantic web notation to the BBC Wildlife Finder, which connects the data to audio and video clips from the BBC Natural History Unit archive. "Creating web identifiers for every item the BBC has an interest in, and considering those as aggregations of BBC content about that item, allows us to enable very rich cross-domain user journeys," states the BBC. "This means BBC content can be discovered by users in many different ways."[19]

The BBC uses the same techniques with its music programming, providing a web identifier for every artist the BBC features. BBC Music links to the *MusicBrainz* music database, *Wikipedia*, and other online content. "BBC Music takes the approach that the Web itself is its content management system," states the corporation. "Our editors directly contribute to Musicbrainz and Wikipedia, and BBC Music will show an aggregated view of this information, put in a BBC context."[20] By adding machine-readable markups to all its content, the BBC has made its resources linkable and discoverable through the semantic web.

A Personal Resource

Berners-Lee wants the semantic web to access not only data from websites, but also from nearly all Internet activity, including social media posts, data generated by the Internet of Things, personal calendars, and online business transactions. The inclusion of personal data will allow the semantic web to be more than a giant library of facts. It will allow machines to create a pervasive computing experience. In an article in *Scientific American*, Berners-Lee and his colleagues explained how the semantic web would help a sister and brother named Lucy and Pete find medical care for their mother and schedule her appointments. The italicized words represent terms defined by the semantic web:

> At the doctor's office, Lucy instructed her Semantic Web agent through her handheld web browser. The agent

promptly retrieved information about Mom's *prescribed treatment* from the doctor's agent, looked up several lists of *providers*, and checked for the ones *in-plan* for Mom's insurance within a *20-mile radius* of her *home* and with a *rating* of *excellent* or *very good* on trusted rating services. It then began trying to find a match between available *appointment times* (supplied by the agents of individual providers through their Web sites) and Pete's and Lucy's busy schedules.[21]

In this example, the semantic web links both public and private information. The doctor's IPA, Pete's and Lucy's calendars, and the location of the mother's home are private. Lists of health care providers, data about health care insurance plans, ratings of the health care providers, and calendars of appointment times come from public websites. All this information is tagged with machine-readable notations. The IPA finds, collects, and makes logical decisions about the data.

Berners-Lee views the semantic web and Web 3.0 as interrelated. "People keep asking what Web 3.0 is," he writes. "I think maybe when you've got . . . access to a semantic Web integrated across a huge space of data, you'll have access to an unbelievable data resource."[22]

Challenges to Creating the Semantic Web

Many computing experts doubt that efforts to build the semantic web will succeed. The Pew Research Center asked nearly nine hundred Internet experts about the semantic web. Forty-seven percent agreed with the statement: "By 2020, the semantic web envisioned by Tim Berners-Lee will not be as fully effective as its creators hoped and average users will not have noticed much of a difference."[23]

The semantic web will be used by machines, but it is being built by human beings, and people often do things to benefit themselves rather than society. Critics of the semantic web believe that human greed will affect how the semantic web is built

World Wide Web inventor Tim Berners-Lee addresses a conference in 2015. Berners-Lee envisions the Semantic Web as capable of accessing personal information such as users' calendars, online business transactions, and data generated by the Internet of Things, as well as public information. This would allow machines to create a pervasive computing experience.

and used. For example, a research team at Ghent University in Ledeberg-Ghent, Belgium, pointed out that semantic notation can be used to send Internet users unwanted advertising known as spam. "Firstly, Spam messages can easily be added to existing resources (e.g., adding an RDF label to an existing resource)," wrote the team. "Secondly, agents will spread these false triples when harvesting them through their automatic update process." The team adds that the semantic web will make it easy for marketers to link all an individual's personal data together to create a powerful marketing tool. "The social networks will be fully linked with the Semantic Web, enabling any piece of data to be connected to anybody's identity. . . . Spam messages become much more convincing by including deep personal information of the targeted user."[24]

There are technical obstacles to making the Internet readable by machines as well. First is the size of the task. Not only are there billions of web pages to mark up, but each page can have many items to classify. In addition, the number of possible classifications is huge. For example, one source of medical terminology alone contains 370,000 class names. Matching data to the correct class names is an enormous task.

Moreover, many terms are vague. A page might use the terms "old" and "young," but how old is "old" and how young is "young"? A person might be described as "wealthy" or "poor," but what do those terms represent in dollar amounts or assets? Machines cannot figure these things out on their own. The best they can do is use advanced forms of computer logic, such as fuzzy logic, to define a range of values for such terms.

Inconsistency is also a problem for the semantic web. The whole point of the semantic web is to combine data from separate databases so it can function as one giant resource. However, data from separate sources does not always agree, creating inconsistencies. For example, one source might refer to Shakespeare as a poet, since he wrote many poems and composed his plays largely in verse. Another source might refer to Shakespeare as a playwright or even a dramatist, since his most important works are his plays. These inconsistencies can pose a problem when a machine tries to make a logical inference. For example, knowing that Shakespeare wrote both *Macbeth* and "Sonnet 123," and knowing that Shakespeare was a poet and a playwright, a machine might incorrectly infer that *Macbeth* is a poem or "Sonnet 123" is a play. A machine programmed with simple logic will fail when it attempts to process inconsistent data. It must employ other logical methods to deal with inconsistency.

fuzzy logic

An approach to computing based on "degrees of truth" rather than the "true or false" logic used in most computing programs.

Overcoming the Uncertainties

W3C identified these and other problems in a report entitled "Uncertainty Reasoning for the World Wide Web." As an illustration of these problems, the authors of the report discussed the uncertainties in Berners-Lee's story about Lucy, Pete, and their mother:

"It is clear that many uncertainties arise in handling this classic use case for the Semantic Web use case. For example, both the provider's and the consumer's schedules may be uncertain, and in traffic-clogged metropolitan areas, the amount of time it takes to get from the consumer's location to the place where the service is rendered may be highly uncertain."[25]

The consortium believes such uncertainties can be overcome with fuzzy logic and other algorithms. The group is continuing to explore and test the most promising methods. "We believe a principled means for expressing uncertainty will increase the usefulness of Web-based information and believe a standard way of representing that information should be developed,"[26] states the group's report.

Some people, such as Berners-Lee and his colleagues at W3C, believe that a unified effort to add metadata throughout the Internet is the best way to achieve a machine-readable semantic web. Others believe that encoding the entire web will be too time consuming and costly compared to the benefits it will provide. They believe a more focused approach that deploys semantic notation in the most content-rich pages will accomplish nearly the same benefit at a much lower cost. Still others believe that a different technology, such as an advanced form of natural language processing, has a better chance of making the World Wide Web understandable to machines. Regardless of the technology used, few would doubt that at some point the Internet will be transformed from a web of documents to a web of data that machines can use to make intelligent decisions and create pervasive computing experiences for their users.

CHAPTER FIVE

Cybersecurity

The World Wide Web Consortium is designing the semantic web to bring together online data about a person's likes, interests, job, calendar, financial information, photos, videos, and location with the goal of creating a pervasive computing experience. Such a storehouse of private information can be very helpful in everyday life, but it comes with risks. If a person's digital profile falls into the wrong hands, it can used for criminal purposes. Keeping this information private is one of the greatest challenges to implementing Web 3.0.

Current Internet Threats

In February 2015 hackers—computer experts skilled at defeating security systems—gained access to private online files within the Internal Revenue Service (IRS), the agency of the US federal government that collects taxes. At first the IRS said that hackers had broken into the accounts of 100,000 taxpayers. A few months later, the IRS revised the total upward to 334,000 taxpayer accounts. In February 2016 the IRS admitted that the hackers copied the data from more than 700,000 accounts.

The hackers used old tax data from the accounts to file new tax returns. They kept the names of the original account holders on the forms, but they changed the bank information to their own. That way the government would send money owed to the taxpayers, known as tax refunds, to bank accounts controlled by the hackers. Each step of filing the return online required the hackers to defeat a new security measure. The IRS software stopped the hackers from filing many fake returns, but at least fifteen thousand made it all the way through the process. As a result, the IRS transferred at least $50 million worth of tax refunds into the hackers' bank accounts.

The IRS believes that some of the information the hackers used to gain access to the accounts—names, addresses, and Social Security numbers—had been stolen in previous hacks of banks or credit card companies. The hackers did not fill out the new tax returns by hand; instead, they used software to modify earlier years' returns to make them look real. The hackers also used a software program to file the thousands of tax returns. A special hacking program was used to compute or guess the answers to the security questions required for online filing. The entire operation was a case of machines talking to machines.

Tax returns contain a great deal of private information about the person filing the taxes. For example, the taxpayer must include his or her Social Security number or taxpayer identification number when filing a return. If the taxpayer has children, their Social Security numbers are listed as well. The return includes the taxpayer's home address, e-mail address, telephone number, place of employment, and bank information. This information can be used to impersonate the taxpayer—a process known as identity theft.

Identity Theft

There are two kinds of identity theft: true name and account takeover. In true name theft, the identity thief uses personal data such as a person's name, Social Security number, and employer's name

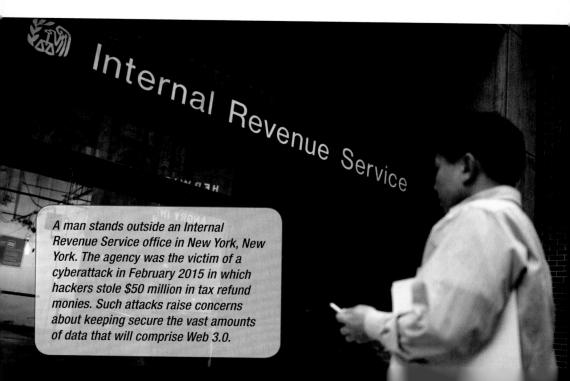

A man stands outside an Internal Revenue Service office in New York, New York. The agency was the victim of a cyberattack in February 2015 in which hackers stole $50 million in tax refund monies. Such attacks raise concerns about keeping secure the vast amounts of data that will comprise Web 3.0.

Peeping Hackers

Imagine seeing pictures taken inside your home posted on the Internet without your permission. That is what happened to a couple in Rochester, Minnesota, who discovered pictures taken in their toddler's room displayed on a website based in the Netherlands.

The parents discovered something was wrong when they heard music coming from the child's room and went in to investigate. The music went off, but the couple noticed the nanny cam in the room following their movements. They used the system's software to see who had accessed the camera. They found an Internet protocol other than their own and traced it to a website in Amsterdam. The couple visited the website and saw thousands of pictures taken inside homes, including their own. "It's not just nurseries," said the mother, who asked not to be identified for the sake of privacy. "It's people's living rooms, their bedrooms, their kitchens. Every place that people think is sacred and private in their home is being accessed. . . . It's pretty sick."

Security expert Bryan Lagard told Yahoo! News that the Minnesota couple's experience is not unique. "People just don't realize that there are websites dedicated to finding open webcams and posting the footage," said Lagard. He cautioned families with nanny cams to be very careful. "It's a wonderful feeling to know that you can check in on your child when you need to," he said, "but like anything else in life, what can be used for comfort one moment can be turned against you in the next."

Quoted in Jennifer O'Neill, "Family Discovers Hacked Images of Child's Crib Online," Yahoo! News, April 7, 2015. www.yahoo.com.

to open a credit card account or a checking account. The thief provides his or her own mailing address so the credit card, ATM card, or checks will be mailed to his or her own address. The thief uses the credit card to buy things or writes bad checks to purchase items until the scam is discovered and the account is closed.

In an account takeover, the thief uses personal information to gain access to the person's existing accounts. The thief then withdraws the funds or transfers them to another account. The user might also make online purchases, such as smartphones or tablets, and have them shipped to his or her address. The thief often pawns or sells these items for cash. The identity thief might open a smartphone usage plan that charges the victim's bank account for calling and data fees. The thief will continue to use the account until its real owner discovers the unauthorized activity.

Not all identity thieves steal directly from the person whose online data has been taken. Sometimes they use the victim's personal data to obtain valuable government documents, such as a driver's license or a new Social Security card. The thief might use the new identity to apply for a legal job or receive government benefits such as welfare and food stamps.

Hackers often sell stolen identities to other criminals who then use the data to make false documents such as fake driver's licenses and passports. The forgers then sell the phony documents to people who are seeking to evade law enforcement, creditors, or others who might be trying to locate them.

Under federal law in the United States, victims of identity theft are not liable for charges made with their stolen credit card numbers. The real problem is that the unpaid bills and bad debts accrued by identity thieves end up harming the creditworthiness of the victims. Companies that compile and report on a person's credit history base much of their data on accounts linked to Social Security numbers. When identity thieves use Social Security numbers to open accounts, purchase items, and then not pay the bills, the bad debt is linked to the victim's Social Security number. The credit rating companies have ways for the victim to dispute items on their credit reports, but removing such items from a credit history is difficult and time consuming.

encrypted

Data that is converted to an unrecognizable form.

A bad credit rating can end up costing the victim money, because many banks use a risk-based approach to setting credit card interest rates. Banks using this approach will raise a customer's interest rate if his or her credit rating goes down, causing the victim to pay more in interest. Many employers consult credit history when hiring, so a bad credit rating can keep an otherwise qualified candidate from getting a job. The same is true for renting a home or an apartment: A bad credit history can keep a person from renting a desired property. A credit rating that has been ruined by an identity thief can take months if not years to repair.

Using Online Data

Criminals do not have to hack into accounts to gain valuable data online. A great deal of data that could be helpful to criminals is posted online every day with little or no security at all. For example, many people post details about their lives on social media, believing that only friends can see them, but this is not always true. Depending on a person's privacy settings, his or her posts might be shared with "friends of friends." These could be people that the person posting the data might not know. Even worse, the friend of a friend could view the post in the company of people who have no connection at all to the friend or the person who originally posted the data. These people can use the online information to plan and commit a crime.

For example, a person excited about an upcoming trip might post a picture of the itinerary for an upcoming vacation. This picture would include the travel date and even the time of his or her departure. With a little online searching, a thief could find the home address of the person who posted the data and then use the travel data to break in to the home when no one is there. Even a post about going for the day to a place such as an amusement park or the beach could provide a burglar with a window of opportunity.

Many people are proud of things they own, and sometimes they share pictures of these items online. If the objects shown have value in the stolen goods market, they might attract the attention of a thief. For example, a gun owner might post a picture of his or

cryptography

The art of protecting information by transforming it into a format that can only be read by those who possess a secret key to decipher it.

Eye-dentification

The growing sophistication of hackers has pushed cybersecurity experts to develop identification systems that are harder to hack than passwords and PINs. A number of devices now use biometric identification to unlock them. Biometric identification requires users to have some part of their body scanned to confirm their identity. Fingerprints are the most common body part scanned, but some smartphone makers have introduced technology that scans unique portions of the eye to verify the user's identity.

Japan's Fujitsu ARROWS NX F-04G features a security system that uses the colored part of the eye, the iris, to verify the identification of the user. More intricate than a fingerprint, the color pattern of the human iris varies from person to person and does not change after age two, making it an ideal biometric marker. The smartphone has an infrared LED and an infrared camera at the top of the phone's front panel. The infrared LED illuminates the iris pattern, and the infrared camera takes a picture of it. If the iris pattern matches with the registered pattern, the phone will unlock. Samsung and LG are reported to be developing iris scanners as well.

Other phone makers have focused on another part of the eye that varies from person to person: the blood vessel pattern in the white part of eye. ViVo, ZTE, and Alcatel have teamed with biometric scanner maker EyeVerify to create systems that scan the whites of the users' eyes to unlock phones.

her gun collection, or it might even be shown in the background of a photo about something else. Since stolen guns have high value to criminals, a burglar might target the gun owner's home.

Some people are motivated to perform bad deeds for reasons that have nothing to do with money, and they can benefit from online information as well. Often these are people who are angry with another person for one reason or another: a jilted ex-boyfriend or ex-girlfriend, an employee who feels he or she was treated unfairly, or a classmate upset by something that happened at school. The angry person might wish to frighten or even harm the person to get revenge for something that happened. Such a person can use social media posts to know where the other person is or plans to be, and then use this data to plan mischief or an assault against the object of his or her anger.

A person who wishes to harm another person can use the Internet to do so. For example, a person might copy another person's photograph from a social media page, alter the image using a program such as Adobe Photoshop, and then post it online to embarrass the person. The same is true for videos. A skilled editor can alter an embarrassing video, making it appear to show the intended victim. The creator of the fake picture or video might even demand money in exchange for not posting it. Such a practice is known as extortion.

Hacking into the Internet of Things

As bad as current Internet threats are, the dangers of Web 3.0 might make them worse, because even more personal data will be shared online. "Things that didn't Internet before are now Internetting," says Gilad Rosner, founder of the Internet of Things Privacy Forum, a think tank based in London. For example, a person might have a digital bathroom scale that shares data with an app in the user's smartphone. This data could help the user monitor his or her weight over time. However, Rosner points out that this data could be hacked. "You might not know where else the information is going," he says. "An insurer would want to know if you're gaining a lot of weight. So would an employer."[27]

The Internet of Things is rife with danger, according to some experts. Tom Kellerman, chief cybersecurity officer of Trend Micro, a software firm based in Dallas, suggested that a hacker could take control of all the devices in a smarthome and use them to spy on the family. "They could turn on the webcam in your child's bedroom and watch them," Kellerman warned. "They could turn on all cameras and microphones in all your devices and see and hear everything you do, or shut down your entire network. This could lead to extortion demands."[28]

Kellerman's warning might seem like the plot of a movie, but

Although parents of young children often purchase baby monitors intended to help them keep their children safe, several couples have discovered that the monitors were being used to spy on their families. These devices, like others in the Internet of Things, such as voice-activated smart televisions, can serve as a means of access for electronic intruders.

such spying has already occurred. In April 2015 a couple living in Lacey, Washington, reported that a camera installed in their toddler's room was being used to watch the family and speak to the three-year-old boy. "For months, my son was telling his family that the 'telephone' was telling him to stay in bed," the mother wrote to television station KIRO 7. The parents did not know what the child meant until the mother heard voices coming from the child's room. When she walked in to investigate, she heard a woman's voice coming from the baby monitor. "Oh, watch this one, she's coming in again,"[29] said the voice. As the mother moved around the room, she saw the camera following her. On another occasion, the parents heard a voice on the baby monitor tell their son, "Wake up, little boy, daddy's coming for you."[30]

Nanny cams are not the only devices in the Internet of Things that can be used to spy on the users. The microphones embedded in voice-activated televisions are capable of picking up not only the users' viewing commands, but also their conversations. Smart TV maker Samsung warned its customers, "Please be aware that if your spoken words include personal or other sensitive information, that information will be among the data captured and transmitted to a third party."[31] The company suggested that the information being gathered will be used to improve the product. However, technology reporter Shane Harris points out, "If the transmission is not encrypted, a SmartHacker could conceivably turn your TV into an eavesdropping device."[32]

New Security Solutions

Securing Internet data is one of the greatest challenges facing computer scientists and engineers today. As more personal data becomes linked in Web 3.0, the need for security will be even greater. It will also be more difficult to achieve, since more devices will be connected to the Internet, giving hackers more possible entry points into a computing network. Cybersecurity experts are busy building stronger defenses against hackers. These defenses fall into four basic categories: firewalls, user account access controls, cryptography, and intrusion detection systems.

Firewalls are the most common Internet security measures in use today. Most firewalls are software programs that inspect incoming data packets before allowing them to pass through to their destination. A firewall might be used as a barrier between a trusted network, such as a LAN, and another network, such as the Internet, that is not trusted. This is known as a network firewall. However, the vast majority of firewalls are barriers between a single machine, such as a home computer, and the Internet. These are known as host-based firewalls. In either case the firewall examines each packet of incoming data to see where it came from and how it was addressed. Some firewalls look inside the packet to see what kind of data it contains. If the packet does not conform to a set of security rules, it is not allowed to cross into the system.

Passwords are the most common form of user account access controls. Most computers and smartphones require the user to enter a password to gain entry into the device. Sometimes the password or personal identification number (PIN) is paired with an

To enhance their devices' security, some manufacturers are equipping them with biometric security systems such as fingerprint readers (pictured). Some experts consider such systems more secure than traditional passwords because they rely on the user's unique physical characteristics.

external device for even greater security. This is known as two-factor authentication. It requires something the user knows, such as a password or PIN, and something the user has, such as a piece of hardware or an identification card. The hardware might be the user's smartphone or a memory stick that attaches to a USB port, sometimes known as a dongle. The hardware contains a code that unlocks the device. By requiring a second form of identification, two-factor authentication prevents a hacker from gaining access to a device even if the password has been stolen or guessed.

Biometric Identification

Some computing devices are replacing passwords with biometric validation systems. These systems rely on the user's unique physical identity to unlock the system. Many smartphones—including the Apple iPhone 5S, 6, and 6 Plus, Samsung Galaxy S6 and S7, Meizu MX4 Pro, and Huawei Ascend Mate7—come with fingerprint readers that can be used instead of passwords to unlock the devices. Mobile payment systems Apple Pay and Samsung Pay both use fingerprint readers to authorize payment. Many laptop computers—such as the Lenovo ThinkPad E440, Dell Latitude 6430u, and HP ENVY TouchSmart 15—feature built-in fingerprint identification technology. In addition, fingerprint scanners are sold as accessories that plug in to PCs and laptops to provide an extra level of security.

authentication

Confirming that something, such as a single piece of data, is true.

Although stopping the hacker from gaining access to a system is the ideal in cybersecurity, it is not always possible. However, hackers can also be stopped once inside the firewall by software programs known as intrusion detection systems. A network intrusion detection system monitors the traffic to and from all the connected devices in a network. If something abnormal appears in the flow of data, the system sends an alert to a network administrator. A host intrusion detection system (HIDS) monitors an individual computer or device. The HIDS watches to see if changes are made in the computer's system files. If a critical file is changed or deleted, the HIDS alerts the user. All packets of data flowing in and out of the device are logged, so the source of the attack can be identified.

Like a chain, a security system is only as strong as the weakest link. Often, the weakest link in cybersecurity is the human being who does not set a password, does not create a strong password, or fails to install updates to make sure security systems are up-to-date. In Web 3.0 it is likely that machines will assume a more active role in cybersecurity, communicating with networks and devices and keeping them up-to-date with cutting edge security technology.

Source Notes

Chapter One: Web 3.0

1. Quoted in Julie Bort, "The 53 Startups That Will Be Huge in 2016, According to Venture Capitalists," *Business Insider*, December 25, 2015. www.businessinsider.com.

Chapter Two: Cloud Computing

2. Quoted in Simson Garfinkel and Hal Abelson, eds., *Architects of the Information Society: Thirty-Five Years of the Laboratory for Computer Science at MIT*. Cambridge, MA: MIT Press, 1999, p. 1.
3. Quoted in Antonio Regalado, "Who Coined 'Cloud Computing'?," *MIT Technology Review*, October 31, 2011. www.technologyreview.com.
4. Quoted in *Peninsula* (Doha, Qatar), "Qatar's Cloud Computing Project 'Has Potential to Earn Revenue,'" November 23, 2011. www.thepeninsulaqatar.com.
5. Quoted in John Markhoff, "Microsoft Plumbs Ocean's Depths to Test Underwater Data Center," *New York Times*, January 31, 2016. www.nytimes.com.
6. Christina Bonnington, "In Less than Two Years, a Smartphone Could Be Your Only Computer," *Wired*, February 10, 2015. www.wired.com.
7. Quoted in Bonnington, "In Less than Two Years, a Smartphone Could Be Your Only Computer."
8. Carolina Milanesi, interview with the author, January 12, 2016.

Chapter Three: Big Data

9. Quoted in Qatar Is Booming, "Research Led by HBKU Scientists Offers a New Way of Identifying Brain Tumor Aggressiveness," February 15, 2016. www.qatarisbooming.com.

10. Preslav Nakov and Marti Hearst, "60 Years Ago People Dreamed of Talking with a Machine. Are We Any Closer?," presentation at SEM 2015, Denver, June 5, 2015.
11. Preslav Nakov, interview with the author, March 4, 2016.
12. Quoted in *Qatar Tribune* (Doha, Qatar), "QCRI's Digital Initiatives Boost Nepal Earthquake Relief Works," May 26, 2015. www.qatar-tribune.com.

Chapter Four: The Semantic Web

13. Alexandra I. Cristea, "Semantic Web," PowerPoint presentation, slide 7. www.google.com.
14. Tim Berners-Lee, *Weaving the Web*. San Francisco: HarperSanFrancisco, 1999, pp. 157–58.
15. Tim Berners-Lee, James Hendler, and Ora Lassila, "The Semantic Web," *Scientific American*, May 17, 2001, p. 34.
16. Quoted in D.C. Denison, "High-Tech Leader Works on Next-Generation Data Web," *Boston Globe*, June 10, 2002. http://cds.cern.ch.
17. Yves Raimond et al., "Case Study: Use of Semantic Web Technologies on the BBC Web Sites," W3C, January 2010. www.w3.org.
18. Raimond et al., "Case Study."
19. Raimond et al., "Case Study."
20. Raimond et al., "Case Study."
21. Berners-Lee et al., "The Semantic Web," pp. 39–40.
22. Quoted in Victoria Shannon, "A 'More Revolutionary' Web," *New York Times*, May 23, 2006. www.nytimes.com.
23. Janna Anderson and Lee Rainie, "The Fate of the Semantic Web," Pew Research Center, May 2, 2010. www.pewinternet.org.
24. Miel Vander Sande et al., "The Terminator's Origins or How the Semantic Web Could Endanger Humanity," paper presented at 11th International Semantic Web Conference 2012, "What Will the Semantic Web Look like 10 Years from Now?," Boston, November 11–15, 2012. http://stko.geog.ucsb.edu.

25. Kenneth J. Laskey et al., eds., "Uncertainty Reasoning for the World Wide Web," W3C Incubarot Group Report, March 31, 2008. www.w3.org.
26. Laskey et al., "Uncertainty Reasoning for the World Wide Web."

Chapter Five: Cybersecurity

27. Quoted in David Lazarus, "Our Privacy Is Losing Out to Internet-Connected Household Devices," *Los Angeles Times*, January 15, 2016. www.latimes.com.
28. Quoted in Lazarus, "Our Privacy Is Losing Out to Internet-Connected Household Devices."
29. Quoted in KIRO 7, "Mother: Hacked Baby Monitor Discovered After Son Heard Voice," April 20, 2015. www.kiro7.com.
30. Quoted in Darlene Storm, "2 More Wireless Baby Monitors Hacked: Hackers Remotely Spied on Babies and Parents," *Computerworld*, April 22, 2015. www.computerworld.com.
31. Quoted in Shane Harris, "Your Samsung SmartTV Is Spying on You, Basically," *Daily Beast*, February 6, 2015. www.thedailybeast.com.
32. Harris, "Your Samsung SmartTV Is Spying on You, Basically."

For Further Research

Books

Tim Berners-Lee, *Weaving the Web*. San Francisco: Harper-SanFrancisco, 1999.

Brendan January, *Information Insecurity: Privacy Under Siege*. Minneapolis: Twenty-First Century, 2015.

Andrew A. Kling, *Cloud Computing*. Detroit: Lucent, 2014.

Patrick Meier, *Digital Humanitarians: How Big Data Is Changing the Face of Humanitarian Response*. Boca Raton, FL: CRC, 2015.

Carla Mooney, *How the Internet Is Changing Society.* San Diego, CA: ReferencePoint, 2016.

Internet Sources

Sanja Kelly et al., *Freedom on the Net 2015: Privatizing Censorship, Eroding Privacy*. Freedom House, October 2015. https://freedomhouse.org/sites/default/files/FOTN%202015%20Full%20Report.pdf.

Barry M. Leiner et al., "Brief History of the Internet," Internet Society, October 15, 2012. www.internetsociety.org/brief-history-internet.

Pew Research Center, "Digital Life in 2025," March 11, 2014. www.pewinternet.org/2014/03/11/digital-life-in-2025.

Jeannette M. Wing, "Computational Thinking," *Communications of the ACM*, March 2006. www.cs.cmu.edu/afs/cs/usr/wing/www/publications/Wing06.pdf.

Websites

Barking Robot (www.debaird.net). Derek E. Baird's blog covering technology news for teens discusses the latest in virtual reality, educational technology, digital privacy, young adult books and entertainment, and more.

iRevolutions (www.irevolutions.org). Digital humanitarian Patrick Meier blogs about using high-tech tools to address disaster aid and development problems. Topics include crisis mapping, satellite imagery, drones, robotics, and big data.

Wired Blogs (www.wired.com/blogs). A collection of *Wired* magazine's science, technology, and culture blogs, including *Gadget Lab*, *GameLife*, *Innovation Insights*, *This Day in Tech*, and *Wired Science*.

Index

Picture Credits

About the Author

Bradley Steffens is a poet, playwright, novelist, and author of twenty-nine nonfiction books for children and young adults. He is a two-time recipient of the San Diego Book Award for Best Young Adult and Children's Nonfiction. His *Giants* won the 2005 award, and his *J.K. Rowling* garnered the 2007 prize. Steffens received the Theodor S. Geisel Award for best book by a San Diego County author in 2007.